PROPERTY OF
ST. CLEMENT'S
LIBRARY
ROSEDALE, MD.

SUN · SIGN

SUN · SIGN

AQUARIUS
by james a. lely

creative education

SUN · SIGN

Published by Creative Education, Inc., 123 South Broad Street, Mankato, Minnesota 56001 Copyright © 1978 by Creative Education, Inc. International copyrights reserved in all countries. No part of this book may be reproduced in any form without written permission from the publisher. Printed in the United States.

Library of Congress Cataloging in Publication Data

Lely, James A
  Aquarius.

  (Sun sign series)
  SUMMARY: Describes the character and personality traits typical of the zodiacal sign Aquarius.
    1. Aquarius (Astrology)—Juvenile literature.
[1. Aquarius (Astrology) 2. Astrology] I. Title. II. Title.
BF1727.7.L44   133.5'2   77-12603
ISBN 0-87191-651-7

SUN · SIGN

AQUARIUS
contents

Your sun sign is aquarius	7
But you're probably not 100% aquarius	14
What you may look like	17
What you might expect — if you are an aquarian	20
School	20
New things	23
Moving	25
Aquarius friendships	27
Health Rx for aquarius	32
Other aquarians like you	35
If your younger brother is an aquarian	36
If your uncle is an aquarian	38
If your teacher is an aquarian	40
Aquarius careers	43
Famous people born under the sign of aquarius	46

AQUARIUS

your sun sign is aquarius

If your birthday is between
January 20 and February 18,
your sun sign is Aquarius.
Your key phrase is "I know."
Your planets are Saturn and Uranus.
Your element is air.
Your symbol is the water bearer.
Your energy is fixed.
Your metal is uranium.
Your flower is the daffodil.
Your stone is sapphire.
Your colors are yellow, white, maroon, beige, and most subdued greens.

Your eyes are focused on the future.
Your life is intense
and different from the norm,
and because you know how different you
    are,

AQUARIUS

you will never pass spoken judgment on another.
You are irritated by the conformity of your fellows,
yet you recognize every man as a "brother."
Your have a deep interest in people
from all walks of life—
whether waiter or senator.

Your impersonal compassion is unequalled.
Courteous and soft-spoken, you may pass through life
neither yawning
nor shaking from excitement.
Your eccentric behavior may tend to confuse and upset others at times.
You possess the wisdom of the ages.
Your eyes are either vague and dreamy
or intently piercing through someone
in whom you are interested.
You love the idea of friendship;
rarely, however, do you make intimate friends.
You always know people
better than they know you.

AQUARIUS

You are best described as a lonely social
 butterfly
because you live in the next age,
and because you will never behave
as the rest of the world does.
You may have elements of genius in you:
the Hall of Fame and Who's Who are full
of Aquarians— and it's not just coincidence.
You may often experience
a highly nervous state
which others may find intolerable.
But you like it there,
and because of Uranus'
influence in your chart
it's in the midst of the nervousness
that your most creative ideas come.

Aquarians are able to win the confidence
of others, which is why people
easily reveal their inner selves to them.
Aquarians spend most of their time
looking into themselves,
wondering what makes them operate as
 they do.
The desire for self-understanding

A Q U A R I U S

often leads to the analyst's couch.
Your opinions will always be frank,
and decisions are made
only after all the facts are in.

You believe in revolutionary changes
but insist on peaceful methods
to effect those changes.
When you think you know what's best for
 them,
you tend to be manipulative
of other people's lives
despite the fact
that you never like to interfere.
You have profound powers of concentration.
Even when absorbed by something
you are also soaking up everything
that is happening around you—
and you surprise people
by telling them so.

You can sense the mood of a room
when you enter,
even before anyone speaks.
Because you instinctively

AQUARIUS

know so much about people,
much of your communication with them is
    non-verbal.
You can spend a quiet hour with someone,
and he or she will walk away exhausted
from exchanging so much information.
After a few minutes of talking to another
you will know that person's deepest dreams
    and desires
and feel a grave responsibility
not to abuse that knowledge.

You are wary of credit cards
and other devices
which tend to bind you
to the world of convention.
You are annoyed by having
to deal with everyday, mundane affairs.
You are honest and will never be caught
    lying;
usually the truth you tell, however,
is what is convenient for you to relate.

AQUARIUS

You are extraordinarily secretive
about your inner core—
maybe because you know how
easy it is for you to see the core of others.
If someone puts a finger on your secrets,
you spin a tight web to keep the person close
    to you—
where the information is under control.
You are socially adept,
and when you entertain,
it is in the best taste,
even if slightly formal or stiff.
You alarm people at times
by your overwhelming efforts to make them
    comfortable.
Certainly they can be alarmed
when you decide that they
are to be studied.

A Q U A R I U S

The Aquarian spotlight is a bright one.
Because you feel no need to conform
to the expectations of others
and because you often have a strong
    influence
on your acquaintances,
you have the potential of being
a powerful person.
You have the obligation of realizing
that even though you are without limits,
most of the world is tightly bound
by convention.
Unlike you
most people are not free
to behave as though
there were no consequences
to their actions.

AQUARIUS

but you're probably not 100% aquarius

Do you recognize yourself? If you were born between January 20 and February 18, you may share most of the personality traits typical of Aquarius. But you probably feel that you don't share all of them. This is not too surprising.

To know that someone is an Aquarius or a Taurus is similar to knowing that he is Japanese, Italian, or Egyptian. A person's nationality tells you something about what the person might look like and how he might think and act. Someone who is Irish might have black hair, a round face and freckles. Someone who is of Scottish descent might be thrifty.

Yet knowing a person's nationality won't tell you everything. Not all people of the same nationality share the same traits. To get a clearer picture of the person, you would have to find out about the person's age, sex, religion, favorite sport and hobbies.

AQUARIUS

In the same way, a person's sun sign can provide some general information. But it cannot reveal all of the aspects of a personality. If an astrologer wanted to know more about a person, he or she would have to find out exactly when and where the person was born. Then the astrologer would calculate the exact position of the sun, the moon and the planets of our solar system in relation to the earth at the moment of the person's birth.

Astrologers believe that human beings are affected by the same energies that cause the sun, the moon and the planets to move in their orbits. They believe that a chart showing the position of these heavenly bodies at the moment of birth can be a kind of blueprint giving clues to a person's personality and potential.

But drawing up such a chart is no easy matter, since the earth, as well as the sun, moon and planets, is constantly in motion. Because of this movement, even identical twins born only minutes apart will have slightly different birth charts, and two

AQUARIUS

Aquarians whose birthdays are ten days apart can be very different indeed.

Interpreting a birth chart is even more complicated than constructing it. That's why many astrologers advise beginners to start their study of astrology by learning about sun signs. Since the sun is the basic supplier of life energy, the sun is a very important factor in a birth chart. Just remember that it's not the only factor.

One more word of caution: it takes approximately 29 days for the sun to move through each of the twelve zones or sun signs of the zodiac. But the exact time when the sun passes from one zone to the next varies from year to year, so the dates listed for any sun sign are only approximate.

If you were born on January 20, you might be either Capricorn or Aquarius, and if your birthday is February 18, your sun sign could be Aquarius or Pisces. In order to tell for sure which you are, you would have to consult an astrological reference book called an ephemeris. After making certain corrections depending on precisely where you were born, you would have to look up

AQUARIUS

your exact time of birth in order to see whether the sun had changed signs by then.

If you were born at one of these turning points and don't have access to an ephemeris, try reading about both signs. See if you can tell which description fits you better.

Your sun sign can't tell you everything about yourself. But it can give you some general characteristics. In reading about your sun sign, you may come to know and understand yourself better.

what you may look like

Your sun sign affects your physical appearance, as well as your personality. Just remember that there are other factors at work and that you probably won't look exactly like this typical Aquarian portrait.

AQUARIUS

The typical Aquarian has:
- softly-focused eyes which appear to be looking at some distant point
- a stature taller than the average
- a slim figure from tensions which burn excess energy
- sharp features, often with the "roman" profile—that is, with a straight, narrow nose
- a head cocked to one side, as if pondering some imponderable problem
- hands quivering with sensitivity—the hands have large knuckles which were once considered the sign of a philosopher
- physical characteristics of the opposite sex—large hips on a man, for example, or well-developed shoulders on a woman
- graceful mannerisms and a fluid walk

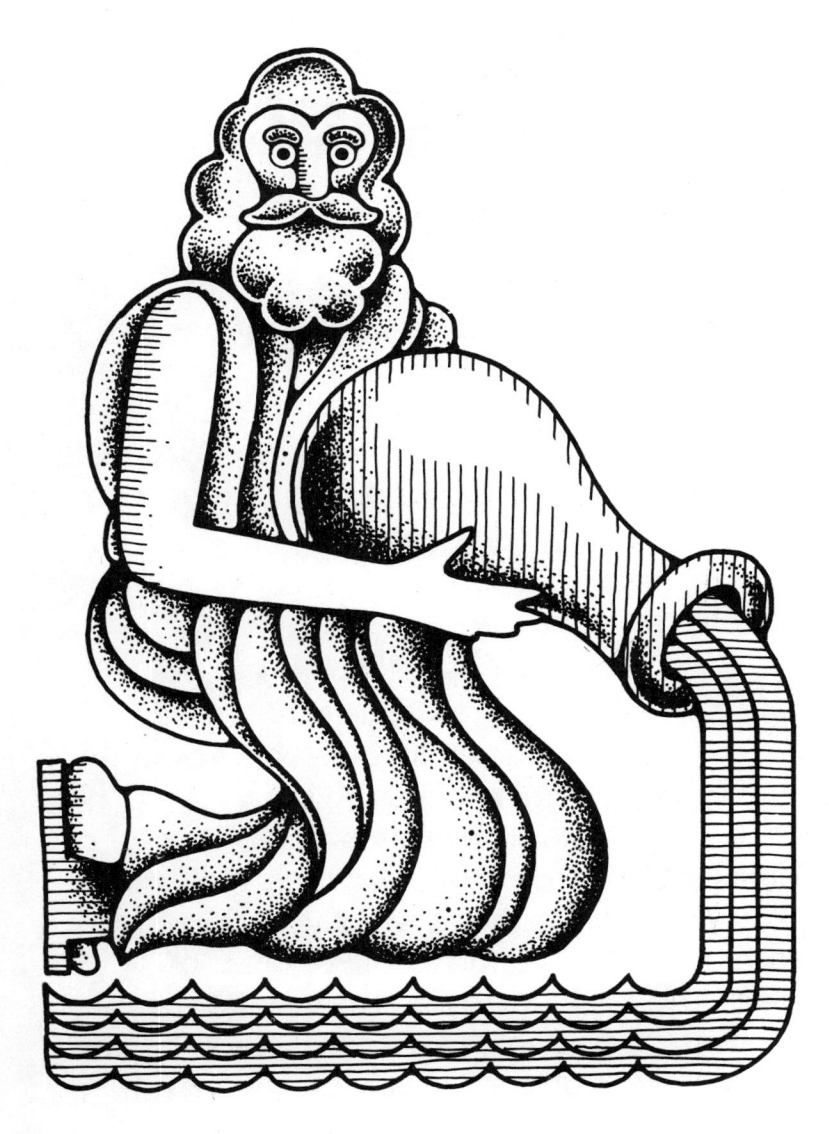

AQUARIUS

AQUARIUS

what you may expect

Your sun sign also affects the way you think and act. As you read the following descriptions of how an Aquarian might act in certain situations, see if you can recognize yourself. But remember that this is a hypothetical person. Don't look for a mirror image of yourself. You will probably only catch glimpses of the you you know.

school

If you're an Aquarian, you may not have a varsity sports letter on your jacket, but you have earned a fistful of blue ribbons from the annual science fairs. Science comes naturally to you. You want facts, not faith, and no other area of study demands so many of them. You are organized and intuitive, often skipping the more conventional steps on the path to

AQUARIUS

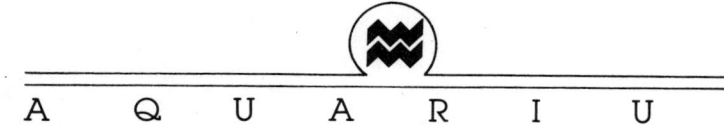

solving a problem. Your project for the fair will not be the same old "Growing Beansprouts in Different Lighting." It will tend to be the very scientific development—from a talking computer to laser photography. You leap on new ideas: you don't look for change as much as you look for the thing no one has ever thought about before.

Like the other air signs, you have a flair for talking— in any language. Your extracurricular activities will probably include the debate team, of which you may be group leader. Besides the gift of gab, Aquarians like to be on top: you think yourself less likely to be bothered by rules controlling others if you are making rules yourself. You take at least one foreign language offered by your school, and you may be studying Greek or Latin on your own so that you can read the classics in original translation. You suspect that you will find insights into them which have never been noticed before.

Because of your natural interest and ability in politics, you will actively seek any and maybe all school government offices,

AQUARIUS

always with your eye on the president's chair. You are an agile campaigner and your intuitive powers whisper to you just what people want to hear. In office you will strive to pass humane legislation designed to make the student's time pass a little more pleasantly. You will arrange to have vending machines installed in the student lounges, or you may be instrumental in getting permission for the students to eat lunch off campus. You will review disciplinary procedures, for injustice of any sort is offensive to you.

If you are an Aquarian, you may have noticed that your teachers tend to look at you strangely. Could it be because of your typical Aquarian unconventional behavior? Do you notice yourself arriving in class late, because the view out of the hall window was too beautiful to miss? Are your papers typed in red ink in order to satisfy your taste in colors? Do you wear plaid cutoffs and walking boots on the first day of spring in answer to your craving to communicate with nature? And what about your whistling during the math

AQUARIUS

exam? These might be some reasons you are talked about in the teacher's lounge during breaks!

new things

New things are the speciality of your sun sign. Saturn and Uranus, your two planets, are a good combination if your goals are improvement, development and invention. Uranus gives the mind liberty and a strong desire to be free and to think in new ways. That is the source of your restless urges and your boredom with the way things are now. Saturn is the controlling aspect in your sign. It lends discipline and order to your wild flights of fancy and provides the control to organize and interpret your futuristic ideas.

It took Edison's incredible imagination to see the implications of his invention, but it took his strong discipline to write down the methods and formulas in a manner that would encourage even more development. Abraham Lincoln's ideas about the equality of all people were far ahead of his time. They

AQUARIUS

were so new that only within the last ten years have we made major changes in our country toward easing tensions between the races. If he had done nothing but think about his idea, imagine what shape the United States would be in today. However, he listened to his Saturn influences and lost his life carrying his dream from idea to reality.

You are always eager to throw away things which no longer interest you. When you have lost interest in you crystal radio set, it will gather dust forever while you take apart clocks or electronic calculators. And it's not unusual for you to put them back together in a different way than the manufacturer intended.

Your craving for new things extends even to your hobbies and entertainments. An Aquarian will invent a new card game, play it and teach it until there is no challenge left, and then completely forget that it existed. Who was the first one on the block to exchange the steering handle on a bike for a car steering wheel? An Aquarian, of course. Even your friends will change regularly, from the most well-behaved book readers to the

AQUARIUS

ones who are the first ones barefoot in the summer and the last ones with shoes in the fall.

You have few attachments to things because your place is with people. That brings us to the next section.

moving

Good news! Your mother's office has transferred her to a new city and your family is going to move in two weeks. You beg to be allowed to come along to look for a new house and to see your new school. Imagine having an entirely new room to call "home!" You are disappointed that you're not able to ride in the cab of the moving van—after all, you've never done that before and it isn't every day you change cities.

In no time at all, you are the talk of the new neighborhood and are always in demand for your many forms of entertainment. Aquarians are social butterflies: you may not ever be really close

AQUARIUS

to many people, but you love humanity in general. Although some Aquarians are athletic, there's a greater chance of finding you organizing a backgammon game than on a baseball diamond. Certainly, you will find a way to join any local club if there is one.

You love disquises and it is real treat for you to use them on your first day of school. You can create a whole new personality for yourself, and the school bus driver will look twice when you get on the bus with your jacket collar wrapped around your face in mysterious private-eye fashion. And when you notice your teachers exchanging glances at your design for a paper jet-liner—no mere airplanes for you!—you will know that you are home again.

AQUARIUS

aquarius friendships

If you are an Aquarian, you will always be surrounded by a number of acquaintances whose friendships will vary greatly in closeness. Very few of them will be intimate friends. You may think that you are looking for that special person who can see forever just as you can, but you really need someone very much in touch with the quieter, realistic side of life. Because so few people can determine what makes you special, whenever one succeeds you try to keep him or her near you. You need a friend who can tell you when your flights into the future are getting too out-of-hand or when you appear to be deceiving yourself. That friend will keep you stable and will make it easier for you to take care of the ordinary details of your life.

AQUARIUS

You will never examine your past, and it is healthy to permit your friend a free hand in explaining it to you. Because you won't usually like what you hear, you may want to lash out and hurt this frank friend. If you do that, you will be a double loser, as you will hurt and lose the friend, and you will be no closer to knowing yourself.

Normally, you are not attracted to people of your own sign because that is an arena of information with which you are already familiar. You prefer to watch people dramatically different from you. They will be of interest to you only until you have found out all there is to know. Then, you will move to new people. Your favorite type of person is one who has gone through many and varied experiences. You enjoy them because you learn from them. In an hour, you can absorb what took years for them to discover. Your instinct tells you when they are hedging while talking about themselves. You will leap on those hesitations as important clues to their personalities.

AQUARIUS

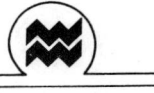

This behavior will leave you alone time and again. You leave behind you a trail of exhausted, confused people who were momentarily persuaded to think that they were everything to you. Despite your charity and warm (although impersonal) affection for humanity, you don't usually see your own actions as unkind. If you do get a pang of conscience now and then, your wisdom seems to whisper to you that there is no other way to behave. You must provide for your own interests first, as you are the only one on whom you can always rely.

Your thorough knowledge of the follies of mankind coupled with the wit of Uranus give you a sense of humor which frequently makes people laugh and then pause to wonder if you meant something else. You are loyal to anyone who has earned your respect, but those who don't know you may judge you as flighty. This is unfortunate for you and for them. You would both benefit from contact with each other.

AQUARIUS

An observer following you through your day would be amazed at how many characteristics you display in a brief period. In one day you will go from being surly upon awakening to lighthearted on your way to a shopping spree. You might be depressed at the sight of an unfortunate person down on his luck, and then angry at the inefficiency of a bank teller. You are charming and flattering at a lunch with a new friend, and then you become callous upon meeting a discarded one.

You can become totally absorbed at the library an hour later. Each of these characteristics is genuine and unaffected. Only taken all together will the observer begin to get a hint of what your motives are. You will always be amazed that people cannot understand you, because you seem so simple and well-ordered to yourself. Remember that this attitude is based on the fact that such things are easy for you and may not be so simple to everyone else.

AQUARIUS

You are a friend in time of others' need. Consoling someone who is struck by tragedy or confusion is part of your healing talent. A headache will disappear in a moment with a touch of your hand and the proper intention behind it. Any person at the end of his rope would do well to seek help from you.

Some of the friends you make will leave angry or shaking their heads. More will stay around, hoping to run into you only rarely. A few will be with you for life. All will be aware that they have come in contact with a person who is very unlike what they had been taught people were supposed to be.

AQUARIUS

health – Rx for aquarius

Aquarians suffer from circulatory problems, and are always too cold in the winter and too hot in the summer. You desperately need lots of sleep, but are often the classic insomniac, lying awake nights with a feverish brain. Your illnesses are sometimes mysterious and are often caused by tension. You must avoid unusual excitement because your health suffers greatly from your frequent mental agitation.

Very few of you will earn your money in professional sports (a notable exception is Babe Ruth). Generally, you don't always see the value of exercise. But if you do physical exercise you feel good about it, because you are suddenly able to think better than ever. If you do take an interest in a sport it will probably be the single-partner type, and you will use the activity as a chance to study your opponent.

AQUARIUS

You are concerned at any injury to your body, and you are upset when you have to stay in bed to recuperate from illness. Despite your reluctance to take care of yourself, you are trim from merely chasing around. You do not like to eat foods which may later cause problems with the heart and circulatory system: eggs, butter and coffee, as examples. You prefer to eat moderately and frequently, so you are sure that you will not get drowsy from heavy stomach activity.

Your reluctance to let your body interfere with your mind is the source of most of your temperate habits. You usually have no philosophical or moral objections but the physical toll is too heavy for you to pay.

It would be sensible to investigate an activity which would benefit both your mind and your body, such as yoga, or discipline yourself into a routine system of morning calisthenics.

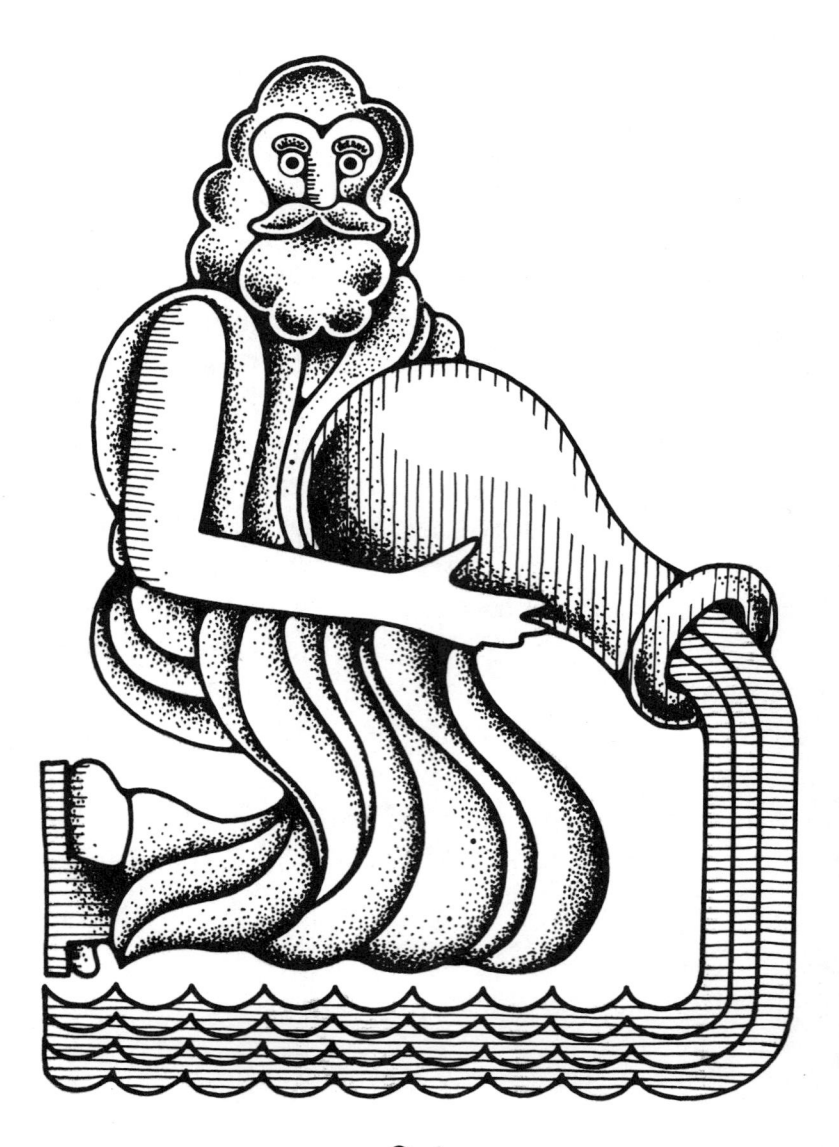

A Q U A R I U S

34

AQUARIUS

other aquarians like you

Some of your Aquarian tendencies will be more noticeable when you're young. Others will become apparent as you grow older. Some traits will be especially evident in certain roles or occupations. See if you can identify typical characteristics in other Aquarians you may know.

AQUARIUS

if your younger brother is an aquarian

He'll probably get under your skin by getting those good grades in school without more than a pass at studying. He will rarely be able to show you how he reached a conclusion—to tell the truth, he won't know, as most things come to him in a flash of intuition. He reads obsessively, and will re-read many times any book which tells him something important about himself. Fiction is his favorite because that is the fastest means to meet many new people. His detective bent may lead him to mysteries, and he will also enjoy science fiction.

A Q U A R I U S

His imaginary friends will be as real to him as live people, and his creative mind will keep him happy for hours merely playing with a pot of dried beans. He is not limited to stereotyped roles, and he may be as interested in baking a cake as in hunting frogs. He will show a preference for quieter friends who can share his dreaming.

He is independent and generally in good humor. At an early age, he learned to get what he wants from grownups and is a delight to those of them who have a sense of humor.

AQUARIUS

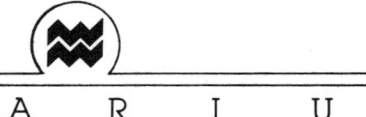

if your uncle is an aquarian

It will be the greatest treat to go to visit him: you can wander around his house for hours, examining mementos and curios from both near and far-off places. Such delights as a running steam engine or a monkey's paw are in the menagerie, as well as books with titles such as "Secrets of the Pyramids" and "Puzzling Incident at the Vacant Windmill." While he is likely to allow you all the time you want to explore and encourages you to ask questions, you can be pretty sure that he is not missing a thing. Before you leave, he will know everything you are up to—especially the things you would never mention to your parents. He is a real friend and will never pass judgment on whatever harmless shenanigans he hears about.

A Q U A R I U S

You may hear your father say that his brother "always was a little odd," and that he is never really comfortable in his presence. Consider that a good sign, because it means that your uncle has retained the freedom of youth and will be a good companion to you on rainy days. Ask him sometime about the time he crawled inside the mammoth pipe organ and the door locked behind him, or about the occasion when he took the French Ambassador to a pizza parlor for lunch. Then sit back and enjoy every word of the tale.

AQUARIUS

if your teacher is an aquarian

The only subject she teaches is human behavior, no matter what the official class title may be. If the course is science she will demonstrate how normal thought processes can be converted to symbols of science. She will make exploring new concepts seem easy and fascinating, because she herself is always wondering at the marvelous order of nature and its works.

The speciality of an Aquarian teacher is showing others how to understand the differences and similarities between people. She can explain what is to be learned from the past and how human nature has remained essentially the same since the beginning of recorded history. It will be easy for her to show you where mankind is

AQUARIUS

headed. Her insights are sometimes so far ahead of her time that she will probably be considered too "radical" by many people of the community. Unpopularity is no problem for her though, as she knows that in ten years everyone will have accepted what she is now saying. If she seems to jump from topic to topic and your head begins to spin, make an effort to listen to her digressions carefully. It may initially appear that she can't keep her mind on one thing, but if you listen with an open ear, you will pick up a variety of information and handy guidelines for use in your own life.

If you have a problem, feel free to approach her and discuss it—she knows what it is already, and may have a ready solution for you. She may not be able to remember your name, because that's one detail she considers to be incidental, a mere label on the all-important package—you.

A Q U A R I U S

42

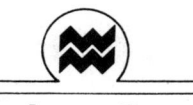

AQUARIUS

aquarius careers

The arts are the expression of mankind, and if anyone knows the human soul, an Aquarian does. Do not look to the corporations for your livelihood. Instead, find expression of your mystical nature using one of your talents. Dancing is natural for you, for it combines mental concentration with physical grace. Furthermore, the exercise will be good for you. Many of the world's finest actors have your sun sign. Unprejudiced and visionary, they can adapt themselves to become nearly any person who has lived.

Acting seems to come naturally from your life-long efforts to disguise yourself. You like disguises because you increase your experience by being someone else and you prevent others from knowing too much about you.

AQUARIUS

Many keen and timely lessons have flowed from the pen of an Aquarian. W. Somerset Maugham, for example, could portray a South Sea fisherman as easily as a Chinese coolie or a Member of Parliament. Each story revealed much instruction on the complex subject of human triumphs and failures. Lewis Carroll lived in the distant future and in a world of imagination. He created stories which provided great escape and entertainment and also carried profound moral lessons.

For a glimpse at the scientific ability of an Aquarian, examine the careers of Galileo or Thomas Edison. Their types, and those of the meditative bent (such as politicians or theologians) face their destiny squarely and do their part for the advancement of mankind.

AQUARIUS

An Aquarian, with natural good taste and manners, is remarkable in a sales force of any type—from selling clothes for a merchant to selling food as a top-grade restaurant maitre d'. Your persuasiveness and ability to recognize exactly what people want even before they do will be richly rewarded.

Aquarians are natural psychics. If you take the time to "school" your intuitive abilities, you could become an expert in some branch of psychoanalysis. It may be as a part-timer in a crisis center or as an eminent leader in the field. After all, is there a better opportunity for you to gather information about the uniqueness of your fellow man?

AQUARIUS

famous people born under the sign of aquarius

Francis Bacon, mathematician and philosopher
John Barrymore, actor
Jack Benny, comedian and philanthropist
Lewis Carroll, writer
Charles Darwin, biologist
Charles Dickens, writer
Jimmy Durante, actor
Thomas Edison, inventor

AQUARIUS

Clark Gable, actor
Galileo, astronomer and generalist
Abraham Lincoln, politican
Charles Lindbergh, aviator
W. Somerset Maugham, writer
W. A. Mozart, composer
Paul Newman, actor
Kim Novak, actress
S.J. Perelman, playwright
Leontyne Price, opera singer
Ronald Reagan, politician and actor
Norman Rockwell, illustrator
Franklin Roosevelt, politician
Babe Ruth, baseball player
Adlai Stevenson, politician

sun signs for young people

creative education

ARIES	•	March 21 — April 20
TAURUS	•	April 20 — May 21
GEMINI	•	May 21 — June 21
CANCER	•	June 21 — July 23
LEO	•	July 23 — August 23
VIRGO	•	August 24 — September 23
LIBRA	•	September 23 — October 23
SCORPIO	•	October 23 — November 22
SAGITTARIUS	•	November 22 — December 22
CAPRICORN	•	December 22 — January 20
AQUARIUS	•	January 20 — February 18
PISCES	•	February 18 — March 20